Schools in Victorian Times

Margaret Stephen

WAYLAND

Victorian Times

Christmas in Victorian Times

Clothes in Victorian Times

Schools in Victorian Times

Streets in Victorian Times

Sundays in Victorian Times

Transport in Victorian Times

How we learn about the Victorians

Queen Victoria reigned from 1837 to 1901, a time when Britain went through enormous social and industrial changes. We can learn about Victorians in various ways. We can still see many of their buildings standing today, we can look at their documents, maps and artefacts – many of which can be found in museums. Photography, invented during Victoria's reign, gives us a good picture of life in Victorian Britain. In this book you will see what Victorian life was like through some of this historical evidence.

Editor: Carron Brown
Designer: Joyce Chester
Consultant: Norah Granger

First published in 1996 by Wayland Publishers Ltd, 61 Western Road, Hove, East Sussex BN3 1JD, England.

British Library Cataloguing in Publication Data
Stephen, Margaret
1. Schools in Victorian Times – History – 19th century – Juvenile literature.
2. Education, Elementary – History – 19th century.
372.9'034
ISBN 0 7502 1829 0

Typeset by Joyce Chester
Printed and bound in Great Britain by B.P.C. Paulton Books

Cover picture: A school group photograph from 1885.

Picture acknowledgements
Mary Evans 7, 8, 9 (top), 11, 23 (top), 24, 25 (bottom), 27; Greater London Photo Library 6, 12 (bottom); Mansell Collection 4; Archie Miles *cover*; National Trust Photo Library (Mike Williams) 6 (top); Northamptonshire Libraries and Information Service 20; Victoria and Albert Museum 5 (top); Richard Wood 5 (bottom).

Thanks to Norfolk Museums Service for supplying items from their museums on pages 10, 12 (top), 13, 14, 15, 17, 21 (top), 23 (bottom), 25 (top), 26, and to Barnham Broom Primary School for supplying the timetable on page 16.

All commissioned photography by GGS Photo Graphics.

Contents

Schools for the Poor

Children in Britain now spend at least 11 years in school. At the start of Queen Victoria's reign, in 1837, many poor children never went to school. Later on, laws were passed to make sure that all children went to school until they were 10 years old.

A Factory School

In early Victorian times, many poor children worked all day long in factories or on farms. They did not go to school, and so they did not learn how to read and write.

Robert Owen owned cotton mills in New Lanark in Scotland. He thought that children should be educated. He started a school at his mills, in 1817, so that children could learn to read and write. They also learned to sing and dance. In the school there were 700 children and 10 teachers. People from all over the country came to see his factory school.

A dancing lesson at Robert Owen's factory school, in 1823. ▼

Dame Schools

Children went to Dame schools if their parents could pay a few pence. These schools were not like schools today. They were often just a room in a house. Some of the women who ran Dame schools could not even read! In Scotland, poor children went to local parish schools.

In 1844, new laws decided that children working in factories should have 6 half-days of schooling every week.

▲ A teacher teaching in a Dame school.

National Schools

Children sometimes learned to read the Bible at Sunday schools run by churches. Some National schools were opened by churches during the week. The lessons were held in church buildings or cottages. The government gave money to help run them. Sometimes new schools were built.

A National school, opened in 1841. ▼

▲ Children today dressed up as Victorian pupils.

Victorian Classrooms

Classrooms in the 1850s were cold in winter and were packed full with children. There were not enough books, and quite often the teacher was just an older child called a pupil teacher.

Some schools taught children only to read, and not to write or do arithmetic. Many of the adult teachers were not trained for their work. Some teachers were trained only for a few days. They often used the cane to keep the children in order.

In the 1860s, people believed that more schools and better schools were needed. There were too many men and women who could not read or write. This was because they had not been to school when they were young.

New Laws

In 1870 in England, and in 1872 in Scotland, new laws were passed so that all children could go to school from the age of 5 years until they were 12 years old.

▲ A London board school. Children do exercises to keep warm.

Board schools were set up because there were not enough National schools for all children. They were paid for by local rates (taxes) and also by the government. At first these schools charged a little money but by 1891 parents did not have to pay.

Compulsory Schooling

Some children still did not go to school. But, in 1880, school was made compulsory for every child from 5 to 10 years of age. Attendance Officers caught children who did not go to school and punished them. Sometimes their parents were punished – they had to pay fines.

School Attendance Officers catch children who should be at school. ▼

By the end of Queen Victoria's reign, in 1901, all children had the chance of a free school place.

Schools for the Rich

Most boys from rich families went to public schools. Their parents had to pay a lot of money. Some boys were sent away from home to boarding schools. This meant they lived at the school and went home only at holiday times. There were not many schools for girls, so they were often taught at home by tutors.

Education at Home

Children of quite rich parents often started learning to read and write at home. They were taught by their mothers or by a nanny.

Parents with enough money hired a governess to teach older girls needlework and French. These girls also had music and dancing lessons.

▲ A governess teaching children.

Public Schools

Eton was a public school and also a boarding school for the sons of rich parents. Boys went there when they were about 10 years old.

▲ Eton College school yard.

Schools such as Eton taught Latin and Greek languages. These were subjects boys needed to learn if they wanted to go to a university when they were older. Boys had a hard time at public schools. Young boys were fags (servants) for older boys, and were often bullied by them.

Lancing College, founded in 1849. ▼

Many new public schools opened after 1840. One was Lancing College, in Sussex. These schools thought that if boys learned religion, sport and good discipline they would become better people. English, science and music were taught. Latin was not as important here.

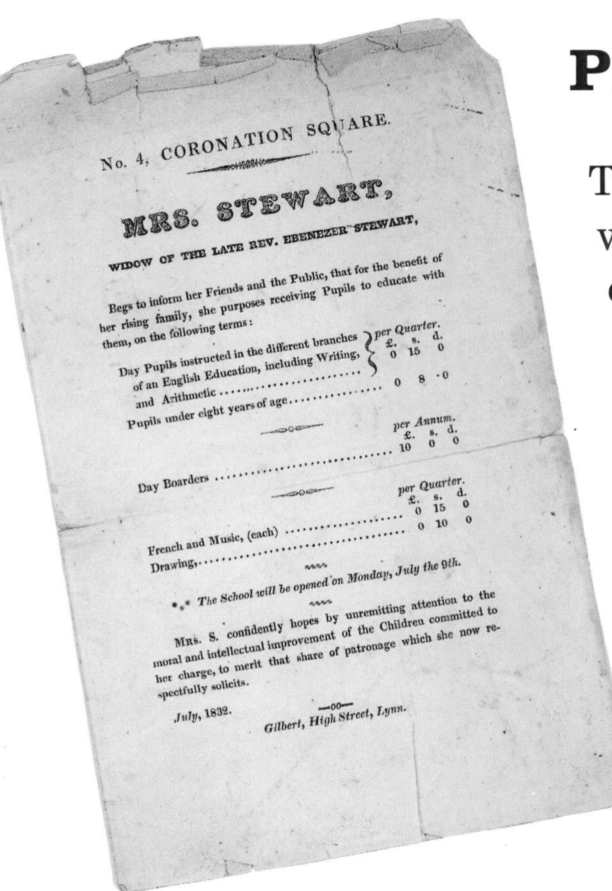
No. 4, CORONATION SQUARE.

MRS. STEWART,

WIDOW OF THE LATE REV. EBENEZER STEWART,

Begs to inform her Friends and the Public, that for the benefit of her rising family, she purposes receiving Pupils to educate with them, on the following terms:

	per Quarter. £. s. d.
Day Pupils instructed in the different branches of an English Education, including Writing, and Arithmetic	0 15 0
Pupils under eight years of age	0 8 0

	per Annum. £. s. d.
Day Boarders	10 0 0

	per Quarter. £. s. d.
French and Music, (each)	0 15 0
Drawing,	0 10 0

*** *The School will be opened on Monday, July the 9th.*

Mrs. S. confidently hopes by unremitting attention to the moral and intellectual improvement of the Children committed to her charge, to merit that share of patronage which she now respectfully solicits.

July, 1832.

Gilbert, High Street, Lynn.

▲ An advertisement for a small private school.

Private Schools

There were also private schools for children whose parents could afford to pay the high costs. Some were good schools, but others were not.

Tom Brown's Schooldays is a famous Victorian school story about Rugby Public School. The headmaster, Dr Arnold, wanted the boys there to learn to become good people as well as to learn their school lessons.

Charles Dickens' novel called *Nicholas Nickleby*, is a story about a school with a cruel headmaster. This story shocked people in Victorian times.

Grammar Schools

Grammar schools had been started in many towns to give free education to boys. By Victorian times, parents had to pay a lot of money for their sons to go to these schools.

At first, only Latin and Greek were taught but later on, pupils learned other languages such as French and German. Maths and science were also taught.

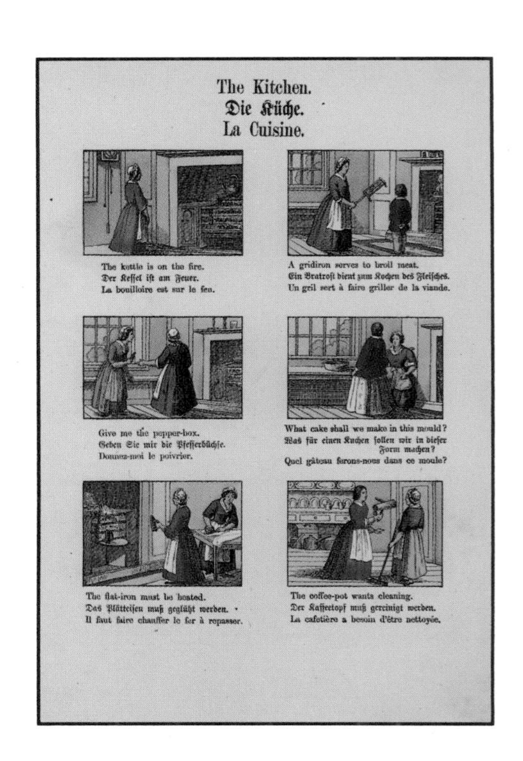
The Kitchen.
Die Küche.
La Cuisine.

The kettle is on the fire.
Der Kessel ist am Feuer.
La bouilloire est sur le feu.

A gridiron serves to broil meat.
Ein Bratrost dient zum Kochen des Fleisches.
Un gril sert à faire griller de la viande.

Give me the pepper-box.
Geben Sie mir die Pfefferbüchse.
Donnez-moi le poivrier.

What cake shall we make in this mould?
Was für einen Kuchen sollen wir in dieser Form machen?
Quel gâteau ferons-nous dans ce moule?

The flat-iron must be heated.
Das Plätteisen muß geglüht werden.
Il faut faire chauffer le fer à repasser.

The coffee-pot wants cleaning.
Der Kaffeetopf muß gereinigt werden.
La cafetière a besoin d'être nettoyée.

A French and German language teaching book. ►

Schools for Girls

Until late in Queen Victoria's reign, most girls did not have the chance to attend school. Women were expected to get married, and look after their children and home.

After 1870, some grammar schools had classes for girls. New private schools for girls opened. There were lessons in art, music, sewing, cookery, elocution (good speech) and manners. Girls were taught these subjects because their parents wanted them to be ready to marry rich husbands.

▲ Schoolgirls from a private school.

The Three Rs

The most important lessons for Victorian boys and girls were the three Rs. They were reading, writing and arithmetic. If you say those words aloud you will hear three Rs. Inspectors visited schools every year to test children in those subjects.

Reading

First, young children learned to read and write the letters of the alphabet. The teacher pointed to a letter on the blackboard. Then all the children chanted the name of the letter. Each letter had its own picture to help children to remember. Often 'a' was for apple.

▼ Infants learning to read.

Later, children learned to read words from the blackboard. They learned by chanting the words over and over again.

Writing and Dictation

▲ Slate with slate pencil.

Children usually wrote on slates. They wrote using slate pencils. The pencils were sharpened to a point.

The teacher wrote on the blackboard. Then the children copied the words or sums from the blackboard on to their slates.

There were also 'dictation' lessons. During these lessons, the teacher read out words or sentences for the pupils to write on their slates. The teacher checked the work and then told the children to wipe the slates clean.

Pen and Ink

Older pupils learned to write on paper, using pens with scratchy metal tips.

Boy or girl monitors filled ink-wells on the desks with ink. When the teacher told them to start, the children dipped their pens into the ink and began to write. They quickly needed more ink when the pens ran dry. They had to be very careful not to drip ink blots on their work.

Pen, ink and ink-wells. ▼

Handwriting

Children wrote in copy-books to learn 'copperplate' handwriting.

They carefully copied the sentence at the top of the page many times on the lines underneath.

◄ A page from a Victorian copy-book. This pupil has not 'blotted her copy-book'.

Arithmetic

Young children learned to add and subtract using counting frames with coloured beads. Older children learned to multiply and divide. There were 'mental arithmetic' lessons where children did sums in their heads. They also had to do money sums.

In old money
4 farthings = 1 penny (1d)
12 pence = 1 shilling (1s)
20 shillings = 1 pound (£1)

Money sums are much easier today using our decimal units of pence and pounds.

Victorian children also had to learn tables of length, volume and weight. The metres, litres and kilograms we use today are much simpler units of measurement to work with.

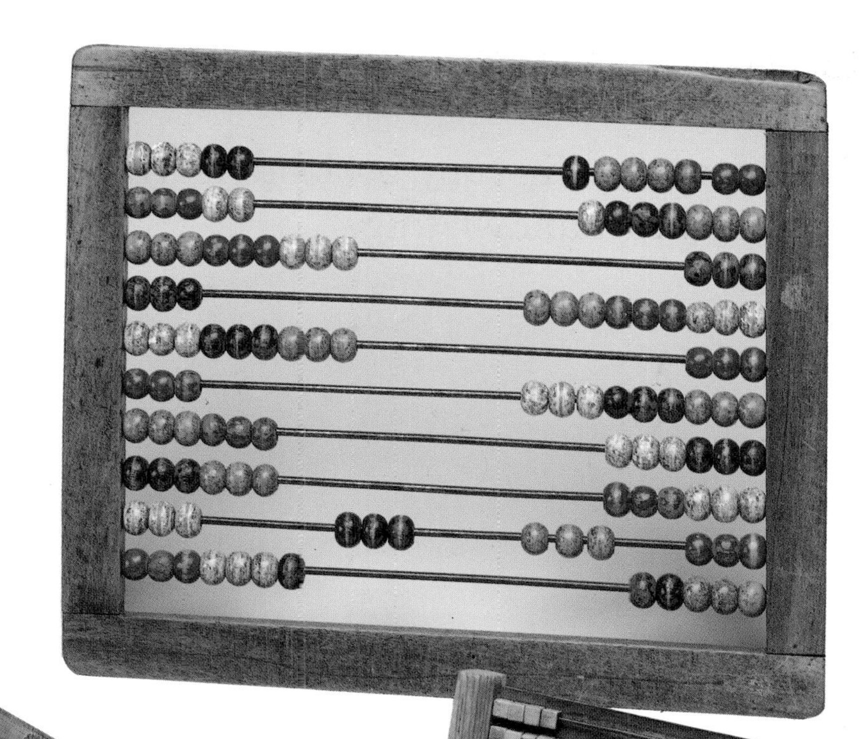

▲ Counting frames.

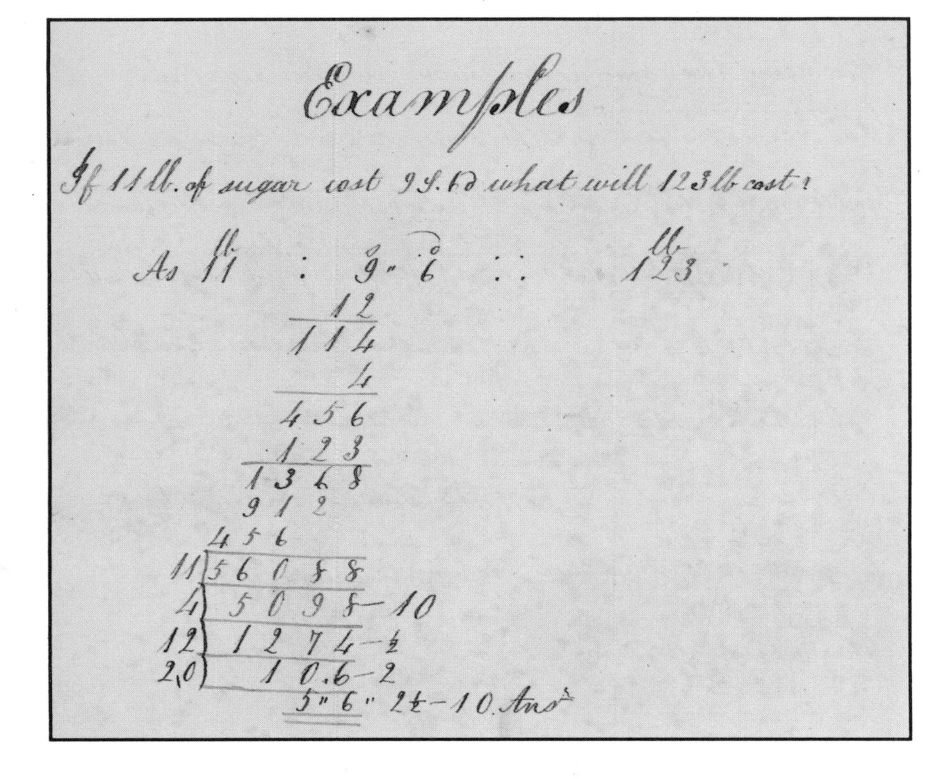

Examples

If 11 lb. of sugar cost 9s. 6d what will 123 lb cost?

As 11 lb : 9 s " 6 d :: 123 lb
12
114
4
456
123
1368
912
456
11) 56088
4) 5098 – 10
12) 1274 – ½
2,0) 10.6 – 2
5" 6" 2½ – 10 Ansr

◄ An arithmetic problem with its answer.

Work and Play

Victorian pupils were not meant to enjoy school. In school today you have many different kinds of lessons, but Victorian children did the same things every day. They sat in rows facing the teacher. The teacher sat at a high desk to have a good view of the class.

◄ A village school timetable, 1874.

This strict timetable was written by the teacher. Every day began with prayers and teaching religion. The children spent most of the day learning the three Rs by repeating what the teacher said and copying from the blackboard.

Sometimes the children learned geography, history and singing. The girls learned how to sew. The boys often learned how to mend boots.

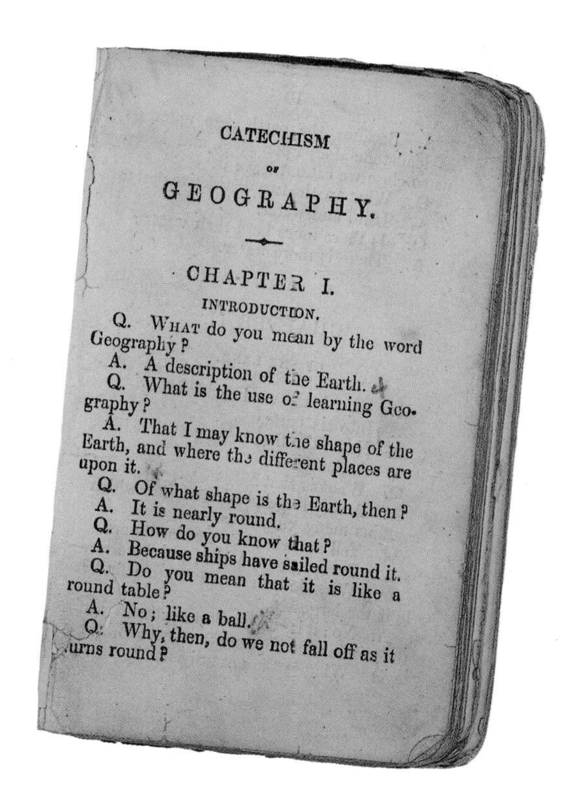

CATECHISM

OF

GEOGRAPHY.

CHAPTER I.

INTRODUCTION.

Q. WHAT do you mean by the word Geography?

A. A description of the Earth.

Q. What is the use of learning Geography?

A. That I may know the shape of the Earth, and where the different places are upon it.

Q. Of what shape is the Earth, then?

A. It is nearly round.

Q. How do you know that?

A. Because ships have sailed round it.

Q. Do you mean that it is like a round table?

A. No; like a ball.

Q. Why, then, do we not fall off as it turns round?

▲ This geography book has no pictures!

Geography

Children learned the questions and answers in geography books off by heart. They learned by chanting over and over again until they remembered. This was called rote learning.

Object Lessons

An object box had trays of small objects for children to look at. There were stones, seeds, shells and fabrics, such as cotton and wool.

The teacher used these boxes, along with sets of books with pictures, to teach 'object lessons'. The children had to learn the names of the objects and what they were. Object lesson cards were put on the wall for children to look at after the lesson.

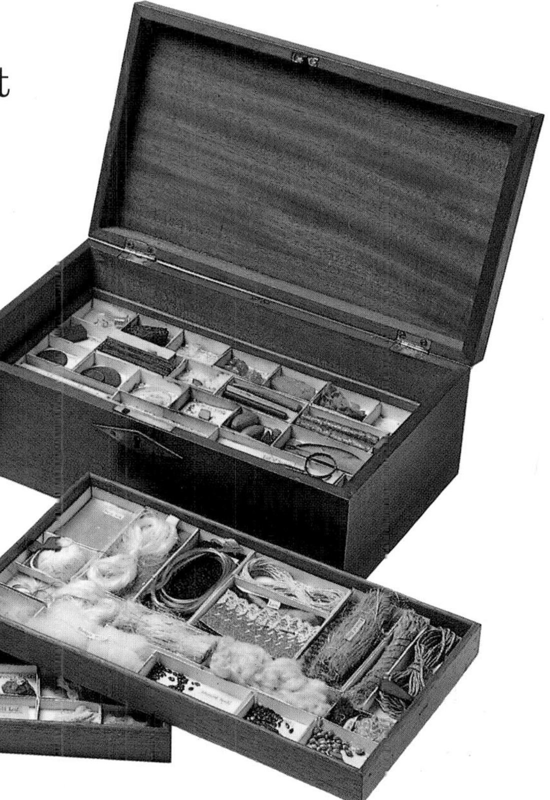

Object box for an object lesson. ▲

▲ Girls doing drill outside in the playground, about 1900.

Drill

'Drill' was what we now call Physical Education or P.E. The teacher shouted orders for all the children to obey at once. On a cold day, drill was done inside to keep warm. Sometimes, it was done to piano music. Teachers could give orders by shouting numbers like this:

One! Stand in desk
Two! Put left leg over seat
Three! Put right leg over seat
Four! Face the door
Five! March on the spot
Six! Step forward

Playtime

Most schools had a small, rough playground for children to play in at playtime.

If the children got dirty there was no tap water for washing. There was also no water for the toilets, which were in sheds outside the school building. The toilets were sometimes just seats over a pit in the ground.

Children played games of tiddlywinks, and hopscotch. They also played with an iron hoop, rolling it around the playground.

Girls skipped to rhymes such as this one:

'George Ware is a very good man
He teaches his children all he can
To read and write and arithmetic
And didn't forget to give them
the stick …'

A Welsh schoolboy with a hoop, about 1900. ►

Teachers and Pupils

How many pupils are in your class at school? Can you imagine a class with 500 pupils? Life was hard for pupils and their teachers. Most Victorian teachers had no training. They had monitors to help them teach huge classes. Later, when classes became smaller, children called pupil teachers helped to teach.

Monitors

Monitors were children who were 9 or 11 years old. The head teacher taught the monitors so that they could then teach the younger children. Each monitor taught a group of children.

This was not a good way to teach children and it was not a good way to learn. Many monitors were not always able to read or write well themselves.

Pupil Teachers

Pupil teachers were boys and girls who had left school. They were over 13 years of age and could earn three shillings (15p) a week as teacher helpers.

They could become teachers when they were 18 years old if they did well.

After 1832, some teachers went to college to train but many were never trained. Teachers were poorly paid but were often given free rooms or a house next to the school.

▲ A pupil teacher's notebook, 1888.

◄ Swannington Country School, about 1900.

Health at School

Many children lived in poor, crowded homes with no drains or clean water. They did not have good food and were often hungry.

Diseases such as measles, whooping cough, typhoid and cholera spread quickly. Children were often ill.

◄ A health inspection.

Public School Boys

Public school boys such as those in the picture went to expensive schools.

They wore stiff collars and square caps. They were expected to be polite and to behave like young gentlemen.

Perhaps the boy who looks unhappy has broken a school rule.

▲ School boys in Eton suits.

The Teacher

Teachers had a difficult time. Many parents had not been to school themselves. They wanted their children to work to make money. They blamed teachers for keeping their children in school. Inspectors blamed teachers if there was anything wrong when they inspected schools.

A card showing pupils making fun of the teacher. ▶

Rewards and Punishments

Your school is probably a friendly place but in Victorian schools teachers were strict. Children were not allowed to talk during lessons. If they were late or badly behaved they were punished. But if they did well they were given rewards.

The School Inspector

Inspectors visited schools to check that teachers were doing their work properly. They looked at the register, the timetable, the equipment and the building.

They tested the children in reading, writing and arithmetic. Children who passed the test moved up to the next standard.

A school inspector testing children. ▼

Rewards

Children who worked hard were given prizes, medals or certificates.

Schools with good test results were given more money than schools with poor test results. Teachers were paid less if their pupils did badly.

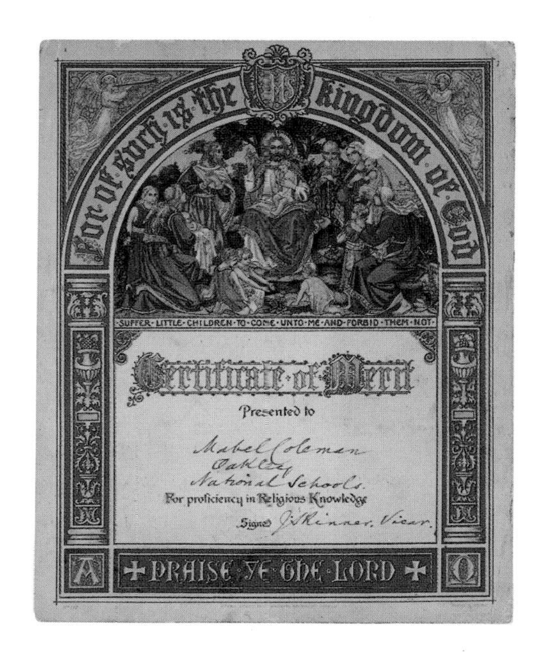

▲ A certificate awarded for good work.

The 'Dunce' of the Class

The dunce of a class was a pupil who could not remember lessons or did poor work. Sometimes the teacher made a dunce stand in a corner, wearing a tall, pointed hat. Pupils were often unkind and made fun of the dunce.

◄ The dunce in the corner.

Good Attendance

Children who were never absent from school were given a medal or certificate at the end of the year. Children were absent when they were ill but others took days off to help on farms or to pick fruit.

A medal for good attendance. ►

Good Results

James Boughton was given this certificate when he passed the 'fourth standard' at the age of 10. He was then allowed to leave school. To pass the test he did some reading, writing and arithmetic for the inspector.

Any child who did not pass stayed at school to try again the next year. Because of this, some children were much older than others in the same class.

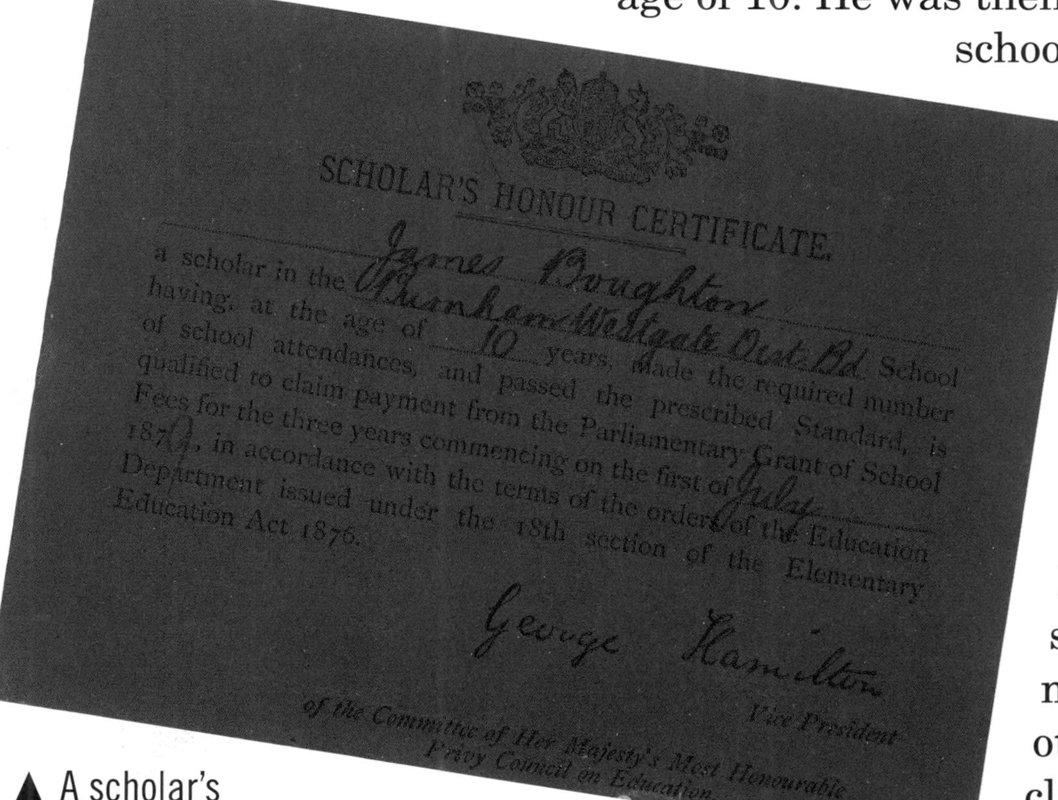

SCHOLAR'S HONOUR CERTIFICATE.

James Boughton

a scholar in the Burnham Westgate Dist. Bd. School having, at the age of 10 years, made the required number of school attendances, and passed the prescribed Standard, is qualified to claim payment from the Parliamentary Grant of School Fees for the three years commencing on the first of July 1879, in accordance with the terms of the orders of the Education Department issued under the 18th section of the Elementary Education Act 1876.

George Hamilton

Vice President

of the Committee of Her Majesty's Most Honourable Privy Council on Education.

▲ A scholar's Honour Certificate, 1879.

Discipline

Victorian parents were strict but so were teachers. Children were caned if they were naughty or if their work was poor at school. In Scotland, a leather strap called the 'tawse' was used to punish pupils. Children expected the teacher to be strict. They thought that a friendly teacher was weak. Children could be cruel.

The writer Flora Thompson tells of pupils who hid their teacher's cane, put frogs in her desk and coughed loudly when she spoke.

A cruel thrashing. ▼

Timeline

BC	AD 0		500	
		43	410 'The Dark Ages'	
Celts		Roman Britain	Anglo-Saxons	Vikings

1800–1830s

1817
Robert Owen's New Lanark Mill School started.

1837
Queen Victoria's reign begins.

1838
Charles Dickens writes *Nicholas Nickleby*.

1839
First school inspectors appointed.

1840s

1840
First training college for teachers opens.

1844
Factory Act says children working in factories must go to school for 6 half days a week.

1846
Pupil teacher system started.

1849
Lancing College founded.

1850s

1853
First large boarding school for girls opens.

1857
Thomas Hughes writes *Tom Brown's Schooldays*.

1860s

1862
'Payment by Results' system starts.

1867
Extra payments made to schools teaching subjects such as history and geography.

1000		1500				2000
1066 Middle Ages Normans		1485 Tudors	1603 Stuarts	1714 Georgians	1837 Victorians	1901 20th Century

1870s

1870
Education Act makes school compulsory for most children in England.

1872
Scottish Education Act passed. School Boards set up in every parish to make sure that there were enough schools for all the children.

1880s

1880
Education made compulsory for all children from 5 years old to the age of 10 years.

1890s

1891
First Special Schools for disabled children started.

1895
Object lessons made compulsory for all infants.

1897
Schools celebrate Queen Victoria's Diamond Jubilee.

1899
School leaving age raised to 12 years.

1900s

1901
Queen Victoria dies.

1902
Britain has a system of free education for all children.

Glossary

Attendance Officers Men employed to make sure that children went to school.

Board school Elementary school run by an elected Board of Governors.

Boarding schools Schools where pupils also live during term time.

Cane A long stick used to hit pupils as a punishment.

Compulsory Demanded by law.

Copperplate A style of joined-up handwriting with thin, sloping letters.

Dame school A small private school run by a teacher in her own home.

Governess A woman employed to teach the children of one family in their own home.

Infants The youngest school children, aged 4 years to 6 years.

Inspectors Men employed to check up on schools, teachers and pupils.

Monitors Older pupils who were put in charge of younger ones.

Nanny Someone who is paid to look after young children.

National schools Elementary schools run by churches.

Parish A local area around a church.

Private schools Fee-paying schools that are run to make money.

Public schools Large fee-paying schools.

Rote learning Learning things by heart by saying them over and over again.

Slates Grey stones that can be split into thin sheets for writing on.

Standard An average level of work that can be done by children at a certain age. Also, a class of children working at the same level.

University A place where young people go to learn more about certain subjects.

Books to Read

Ross, S. *Our Schools* (Wayland, 1992)

Steel, A. *Victorian Children* (Wayland, 1990)

Tanner, G. and Wood, T. *History Mysteries – At School* (A & C Black, 1992)

Places to Visit

Many museums have displays about Victorian schools. Sometimes it is possible to touch Victorian objects or take part in role play sessions. The museums listed all have reconstructed Victorian classrooms.

England

Cambridgeshire: Centre For Environmental Education, Stibbington, Peterborough, PE8 6LP. Tel. 01780 782386

Cheshire: Heritage Centre, Roe Street, Macclesfield, SK11 6UT. Tel. 01625 613210

County Durham: North of England Open Air Museum, Beamish, DH9 0RG. Tel. 01207 231811

Hertfordshire: British Schools Museum, Queen Street, Hitchin, SG4 9TS. Tel. 01462 420144

Lancashire: Museum of Childhood, Lancaster, LA1 1YS. Tel. 01524 32808

London: Ragged School Museum, Copperfield Road, London, E3 4RR. Tel. 0181 9806405

Merseyside: Museum of Labour History, Islington, L3 8EE. Tel. 0151 2070001

Norfolk: Gressenhall Rural Life Museum, Dereham, NR20 4DR. Tel. 01362 860563

Oxfordshire: Fringford Old School, Woodstock, OX7 1SN. Tel. 01993 811456

Quarry Bank Mill, Styal, SK9 4LA. Tel. 01625 527468

Staffordshire: County Museum, Shugborough, ST17 0XB. Tel. 01889 881388

Sussex: Weald and Downland Open Air Museum, Singleton, PO18 0EU. Tel. 01243 811348

Warwickshire: St John's House Museum, Warwick, CV34 4NF. Tel. 01926 412034

Wigan Pier Heritage Centre, Wigan, WN3 4EU. Tel. 01942 323666

Worcestershire: Tudor House Museum, Worcester, WR1 2NA. Tel. 01905 355071

Yorkshire: Industrial Museum, Armley, LS12 2QF. Tel. 01532 797326

Scotland

Angus: Angus Folk Museum, Glamis, Forfar, DD8 1RT. Tel. 01307 464123

Lothian: History of Education Centre, East London Street, Edinburgh, EH7 4BW. Tel. 0131 5564224

Glasgow: Museum of Education, Scotland Street, G5 8QB. Tel. 0141 4291202

Lanark: New Lanark Mills, ML11 9DB. Tel. 01555 661345

Wales

Cardiff: Welsh Folk Museum, St Fagans, CF5 6XB. Tel. 01222 569441

Northern Ireland

County Down: Ulster Folk and Transport Museum, Holywood, BT18 0EU. Tel. 012317 5411

County Tyrone: Ulster American Folk Park, Castletown, Omagh, BT78 5QY. Tel. 01662 243292

Index